GRACE to Thrive

LIVING VICTORIOUSLY

ONE SCRIPTURE AT A TIME

30-DAY JOURNAL

This scripture writing journal belongs to:

_____

Watersprings
PUBLISHING

Grace to Thrive, Scripture Writing Journal

Published by Watersprings Media House, LLC.

P.O. Box 1284

Olive Branch, MS 38654

www.waterspringsmedia.com

© 2018 Copyrights Watersprings Media House. All rights reserved.

No portion of this book may be reproduced, stored in a retrieval system or transmitted in any form or by any means (electronic, mechanical, photocopy, recording, scanning, or other), except for brief quotations in critical reviews of articles, without the prior written permission of the writer.

Scripture quotations credited to NIV are from the Holy Bible, New International Version. Copyright © 1973, 1978, 1984, 2011 by Biblica, Inc. Used by permission. All rights reserved worldwide.

ISBN 13: 978-1-948877-10-7

Introduction

Some of us who have endured tragedy, loss or the trials of life will eventually come to a place of realization that we have survived. You survived the tests, survived the attacks, survived the sickness, survived the rocky relationships, etc. When you know what you have survived you can truly celebrate and live victoriously. However, there are some people that remain in survival mode. In survival mode, you are defensive, walls are up and safety mechanisms are high. You find yourself mistrusting everyone and self-isolating. In order to live victoriously you have to transition from survival mode to thriving mode. In this mode, you are not surviving but thriving, growing and prospering. This is the moment you re-define your bliss, maintain your peace and live victoriously.

How to Use this Scripture Writing Journal

As you use this journal, for the next 30 days, your faith will grow stronger and your hope deeper. Hope sustains us and fuels our faith especially during our most difficult days. I encourage you to allow the Spirit of the living God to breathe into you every day. This journal provides four sections each day to write from the provided scripture:

Write - As you write the Word of God, allow it to penetrate your heart and mind afresh, even if it is a familiar scripture.

Listen - Listen to your heart, good, bad or indifferent and simply write. Then listen to the heart of God through that scripture and/or in that moment and write what you hear or what you understand from that scripture.

Pray - Next, take a moment to reconcile your heart and thoughts with God's words, then write a prayer from your heart. Acknowledge who God is and where you are, thanking and asking God for what you need in that moment.

My Affirmation - I've discovered that speaking positively, declaring and decreeing words of faith and affirmation will encourage you and shift your thinking. At the end of each entry write a personal affirmation. Take it a step further, put in on a post-it note, your cell phone screen or make it your daily hashtag on social media. Speak it and repeat it until you feel a difference in your spirit.

Athena C. Shack
#IAMVICTORIOUS

*Thou hast enlarged my steps under me,
that my feet did not slip.*

Psalms 18:36 KJV

Write the Word

Listen to the Word

Pray the Word

My Affirmation

*Let the redeemed of the Lord
tell their story – those he redeemed
from the hand of the foe.*

Psalm 107:2

Write the Word

Listen to the Word

Pray the Word

My Affirmation

*And the God of all grace,
who called you to his eternal glory
in Christ, after you have suffered a little
while, will himself restore you and make
you strong, firm and steadfast.*

1 Peter 5:10

Write the Word

Listen to the Word

Pray the Word

My Affirmation

*I will repay you for the years
the locusts have eaten –
the great locust and the young locust,
the other locusts and the locust swarm –
my great army that I sent among you.*

Joel 2:25

Write the Word

Listen to the Word

Pray the Word

My Affirmation

But he said to me,
"My grace is sufficient for you, for my
power is made perfect in weakness."
2 Corinthians 12:9a

Write the Word

Listen to the Word

Pray the Word

My Affirmation

Being confident of this, that he who began a good work in you will carry it on to completion until the day of Christ Jesus.

Philippians 1:6

Write the Word

Listen to the Word

Pray the Word

My Affirmation

*For no matter how many promises
God has made, they are "Yes" in Christ.
And so through him the "Amen"
is spoken by us to the glory of God.*

2 Corinthians 1:20

Write the Word

Listen to the Word

Pray the Word

My Affirmation

Rejoice always, pray continually, give thanks in all circumstances; for this is God's will for you in Christ Jesus.

1 Thessalonians 5:16-18

Write the Word

Listen to the Word

Pray the Word

My Affirmation

*...continue to live your lives in him,
rooted and built up in him, strengthened
in the faith as you were taught,
and overflowing with thankfulness.*

Colossians 2:6b-7

Write the Word

Listen to the Word

Pray the Word

My Affirmation

For it is God who works in you to will and to act in order to fulfill his good purpose.

Philippians 2:13

Listen to the Word

Pray the Word

My Affirmation

*I pray that the eyes of your heart
may be enlightened in order that
you may know the hope to which
he has called you, the riches of his
glorious inheritance in his holy people...*

Ephesians 1:18

Write the Word

Listen to the Word

Pray the Word

My Affirmation

*Devote yourselves to prayer,
being watchful and thankful.*

Colossians 4:2

Write the Word

Listen to the Word

Pray the Word

My Affirmation

Now this I know: The Lord gives victory to his anointed. He answers him from his heavenly sanctuary with the victorious power of his right hand.

Psalm 20:6

Write the Word

Listen to the Word

Pray the Word

My Affirmation

*The lions may grow weak and hungry,
but those who seek the Lord
lack no good thing.*

Psalm 34:10

Write the Word

Listen to the Word

Pray the Word

My Affirmation

*The Lord makes firm the steps
of the one who delights in him;
though he may stumble, he will not fall,
for the Lord upholds him with his hand.*

Psalm 37:23-24

Write the Word

Listen to the Word

Pray the Word

My Affirmation

In you, Lord my God, I put my trust.
Psalm 25:1

Write the Word

Listen to the Word

Pray the Word

My Affirmation

... to be made new in the attitude of your minds; and to put on the new self, created to be like God in true righteousness and holiness.

Ephesians 4:23-24

Write the Word

Listen to the Word

Pray the Word

My Affirmation

*Take delight in the Lord,
and he will give you
the desires of your heart.*

Psalm 37:4

Write the Word

Listen to the Word

Pray the Word

My Affirmation

*May God himself, the God of peace,
sanctify you through and through.
May your whole spirit, soul and body
be kept blameless at the coming
of our Lord Jesus Christ.*

1 Thessalonians 5:23

Write the Word

Listen to the Word

Pray the Word

My Affirmation

> "For in him we live and move and have our being." As some of your own poets have said, "We are his offspring."
>
> Acts 17:28

Write the Word

Listen to the Word

Pray the Word

My Affirmation

*Let us not become weary in doing good,
for at the proper time we will reap
a harvest if we do not give up.*

Galatians 6:9

Write the Word

Listen to the Word

Pray the Word

My Affirmation

*Therefore, with minds that are alert
and fully sober, set your hope on the grace
to be brought to you when Jesus Christ
is revealed at his coming.*

1 Peter 1:13

Write the Word

Listen to the Word

Pray the Word

My Affirmation

*You will keep in perfect peace
those whose minds are steadfast,
because they trust in you.*

Isaiah 26:3

Write the Word

Listen to the Word

Pray the Word

My Affirmation

*Set your minds on things above,
not on earthly things.*

Colossians 3:2

Write the Word

Listen to the Word

Pray the Word

My Affirmation

Whoever dwells in the shelter of the Most High will rest in the shadow of the Almighty.

Psalm 91:1

Write the Word

Listen to the Word

Pray the Word

My Affirmation

But thanks be to God!
He gives us the victory
through our Lord Jesus Christ.

1 Corinthians 15:57

Write the Word

Listen to the Word

Pray the Word

My Affirmation

For the Lord your God is the one who goes with you to fight for you against your enemies to give you victory.

Deuteronomy 20:4

Write the Word

Listen to the Word

Pray the Word

My Affirmation

Let the peace of Christ rule in your hearts, since as members of one body you were called to peace. And be thankful.

Colossians 3:15

Write the Word

Listen to the Word

Pray the Word

My Affirmation

For everyone born of God overcomes the world. This is the victory that has overcome the world, even our faith.

1 John 5:4

Write the Word

Listen to the Word

Pray the Word

My Affirmation

Finally, be strong in the Lord and in his mighty power.

Ephesians 6:10

Write the Word

Listen to the Word

Pray the Word

My Affirmation

www.ingramcontent.com/pod-product-compliance
Lightning Source LLC
Chambersburg PA
CBHW060046230426
43661CB00004B/672